MW00846066
LARGE PRINT PASSWORD LOGBOOK
LARGE PRINT PASSWORD LOGBOOK
INTERNET LOGIN & PASSWORD ORGANIZER: FLOWERS
COPYRIGHT © 2017 BY SYNCHRONISTA LLC. ALL RIGHTS RESERVED.
PUBLISHED BY SYNCHRONISTA LLC – GILBERT, ARIZONA, USA
SYNCHRONISTA® IS A REGISTERED TRADEMARK OF SYNCHRONISTA LLC
WEB: SYNCHRONISTA.COM
SEE MORE OF OUR BOOKS AT MYRIA.COM/SHOP

{ NOTES }

- In addition to space to store information about the sites you visit, we have also included pages to write down your modem/router setup, your internet service provider details, email login info, and registry numbers for software programs.

- There are between 2 and 6 pages for every letter, except for **U&V** and **X, Y & Z**, which share pages. There are also two pages at the beginning of the index for website addresses that start with numbers.

- Every log page has space for four websites, so between the alphanumeric log pages and the two favorite site pages, there's room to store data for more than 400 sites.

- We have included two lines for your passwords so you have space to write the new information down when you change them periodically. If you need more space, there is also room below under "notes."

- Each letter/number page features between 1 and 6 dots in the lower outer corners to let you know which page of that letter you're on. (Example: Page 3 of letter A will feature 3 dots, page 4 of letter S will have 4 dots.)

- See the index on page 3 to see exactly where the first page of each section begins.

{ CONTENTS }

ALPHANUMERIC PAGE INDEX

FAVORITE SITES

SITE NAME:

WEB ADDRESS:

LOGIN/USER:

PASSWORD:

NOTES:

SITE NAME:

WEB ADDRESS:

LOGIN/USER:

PASSWORD:

NOTES:

SITE NAME:

WEB ADDRESS:

LOGIN/USER:

PASSWORD:

NOTES:

SITE NAME:

WEB ADDRESS:

LOGIN/USER:

PASSWORD:

NOTES:

SITE NAME:

WEB ADDRESS:

LOGIN/USER:

PASSWORD:

NOTES:

SITE NAME:

WEB ADDRESS:

LOGIN/USER:

PASSWORD:

NOTES:

SITE NAME:

WEB ADDRESS:

LOGIN/USER:

PASSWORD:

NOTES:

SITE NAME:

WEB ADDRESS:

LOGIN/USER:

PASSWORD:

NOTES:

INTERNET & EMAIL SETUP

● INTERNET SERVICE PROVIDER

ACCOUNT NUMBER:

WEBSITE:

USERNAME:

PASSWORD:

TECH SUPPORT #:

CUSTOMER SERVICE #:

OTHER:

● EMAIL SERVER ACCESS

YOUR EMAIL ADDRESS:

INCOMING MAIL SETTINGS ☐ **POP3** ☐ **IMAP**

SERVER NAME:

PORT #:

OUTGOING MAIL SETTINGS (SMTP)

SERVER NAME:

PORT #:

USERNAME:

PASSWORD:

● WEBMAIL ACCESS

WEBSITE:

USERNAME:

PASSWORD:

● MODEM

MODEL/SERIAL NUMBER:

MAC ADDRESS:

ADMIN IP/URL:

USERNAME:

PASSWORD:

WAN IP:

DNS (1): DNS (2):

OTHER:

● WIRELESS (WI-FI)

NETWORK NAME (SSID):

CHANNEL: ENCRYPTION TYPE:

PASSWORD (NETWORK KEY):

ADMIN IP/URL:

USERNAME:

PASSWORD:

WEP KEY:

WPA/WPA2 KEY/PASSPHRASE:

OTHER:

NOTES:

SOFTWARE LICENSES

PROGRAM: DATE:

LICENSE KEY:

DOWNLOAD/SITE:

USERNAME:

PASSWORD:

PROGRAM: DATE:

LICENSE KEY:

DOWNLOAD/SITE:

USERNAME:

PASSWORD:

PROGRAM: DATE:

LICENSE KEY:

DOWNLOAD/SITE:

USERNAME:

PASSWORD:

PROGRAM: DATE:

LICENSE KEY:

DOWNLOAD/SITE:

USERNAME:

PASSWORD:

SOFTWARE LICENSES

PROGRAM: DATE:

LICENSE KEY:

DOWNLOAD/SITE:

USERNAME:

PASSWORD:

PROGRAM: DATE:

LICENSE KEY:

DOWNLOAD/SITE:

USERNAME:

PASSWORD:

PROGRAM: DATE:

LICENSE KEY:

DOWNLOAD/SITE:

USERNAME:

PASSWORD:

PROGRAM: DATE:

LICENSE KEY:

DOWNLOAD/SITE:

USERNAME:

PASSWORD:

1
2
3
4
5
6
7
8
9
0
•

SITE NAME:

WEB ADDRESS:

LOGIN/USER:

PASSWORD:

NOTES:

SITE NAME:

WEB ADDRESS:

LOGIN/USER:

PASSWORD:

NOTES:

SITE NAME:

WEB ADDRESS:

LOGIN/USER:

PASSWORD:

NOTES:

SITE NAME:

WEB ADDRESS:

LOGIN/USER:

PASSWORD:

NOTES:

SITE NAME:

WEB ADDRESS:

LOGIN/USER:

PASSWORD:

NOTES:

SITE NAME:

WEB ADDRESS:

LOGIN/USER:

PASSWORD:

NOTES:

SITE NAME:

WEB ADDRESS:

LOGIN/USER:

PASSWORD:

NOTES:

SITE NAME:

WEB ADDRESS:

LOGIN/USER:

PASSWORD:

NOTES:

1 2 3 4 5 6 7 8 9 0 • •

A A A A A

SITE NAME:

WEB ADDRESS:

LOGIN/USER:

PASSWORD:

NOTES:

SITE NAME:

WEB ADDRESS:

LOGIN/USER:

PASSWORD:

NOTES:

SITE NAME:

WEB ADDRESS:

LOGIN/USER:

PASSWORD:

NOTES:

SITE NAME:

WEB ADDRESS:

LOGIN/USER:

PASSWORD:

NOTES:

SITE NAME:
WEB ADDRESS:
LOGIN/USER:
PASSWORD:

NOTES:

SITE NAME:
WEB ADDRESS:
LOGIN/USER:
PASSWORD:

NOTES:

SITE NAME:
WEB ADDRESS:
LOGIN/USER:
PASSWORD:

NOTES:

SITE NAME:
WEB ADDRESS:
LOGIN/USER:
PASSWORD:

NOTES:

A

A

A

A

A

SITE NAME:
WEB ADDRESS:
LOGIN/USER:
PASSWORD:

NOTES:

SITE NAME:
WEB ADDRESS:
LOGIN/USER:
PASSWORD:

NOTES:

SITE NAME:
WEB ADDRESS:
LOGIN/USER:
PASSWORD:

NOTES:

SITE NAME:
WEB ADDRESS:
LOGIN/USER:
PASSWORD:

NOTES:

SITE NAME:

WEB ADDRESS:

LOGIN/USER:

PASSWORD:

NOTES:

SITE NAME:

WEB ADDRESS:

LOGIN/USER:

PASSWORD:

NOTES:

SITE NAME:

WEB ADDRESS:

LOGIN/USER:

PASSWORD:

NOTES:

SITE NAME:

WEB ADDRESS:

LOGIN/USER:

PASSWORD:

NOTES:

A

A

A

A

A

A

SITE NAME:
WEB ADDRESS:
LOGIN/USER:
PASSWORD:

NOTES:

SITE NAME:
WEB ADDRESS:
LOGIN/USER:
PASSWORD:

NOTES:

SITE NAME:
WEB ADDRESS:
LOGIN/USER:
PASSWORD:

NOTES:

SITE NAME:
WEB ADDRESS:
LOGIN/USER:
PASSWORD:

NOTES:

A

SITE NAME:

WEB ADDRESS:

LOGIN/USER:

PASSWORD:

NOTES:

SITE NAME:

WEB ADDRESS:

LOGIN/USER:

PASSWORD:

NOTES:

SITE NAME:

WEB ADDRESS:

LOGIN/USER:

PASSWORD:

NOTES:

SITE NAME:

WEB ADDRESS:

LOGIN/USER:

PASSWORD:

NOTES:

B

B

B

B

B

SITE NAME:

WEB ADDRESS:

LOGIN/USER:

PASSWORD:

NOTES:

SITE NAME:

WEB ADDRESS:

LOGIN/USER:

PASSWORD:

NOTES:

SITE NAME:

WEB ADDRESS:

LOGIN/USER:

PASSWORD:

NOTES:

SITE NAME:

WEB ADDRESS:

LOGIN/USER:

PASSWORD:

NOTES:

B

SITE NAME:

WEB ADDRESS:

LOGIN/USER:

PASSWORD:

NOTES:

SITE NAME:

WEB ADDRESS:

LOGIN/USER:

PASSWORD:

NOTES:

SITE NAME:

WEB ADDRESS:

LOGIN/USER:

PASSWORD:

NOTES:

SITE NAME:

WEB ADDRESS:

LOGIN/USER:

PASSWORD:

NOTES:

B

B

B

B

B

SITE NAME:

WEB ADDRESS:

LOGIN/USER:

PASSWORD:

NOTES:

SITE NAME:

WEB ADDRESS:

LOGIN/USER:

PASSWORD:

NOTES:

SITE NAME:

WEB ADDRESS:

LOGIN/USER:

PASSWORD:

NOTES:

SITE NAME:

WEB ADDRESS:

LOGIN/USER:

PASSWORD:

NOTES:

SITE NAME:

WEB ADDRESS:

LOGIN/USER:

PASSWORD:

NOTES:

SITE NAME:

WEB ADDRESS:

LOGIN/USER:

PASSWORD:

NOTES:

SITE NAME:

WEB ADDRESS:

LOGIN/USER:

PASSWORD:

NOTES:

SITE NAME:

WEB ADDRESS:

LOGIN/USER:

PASSWORD:

NOTES:

B B B B B

C

C

C

C

C

SITE NAME:

WEB ADDRESS:

LOGIN/USER:

PASSWORD:

NOTES:

SITE NAME:

WEB ADDRESS:

LOGIN/USER:

PASSWORD:

NOTES:

SITE NAME:

WEB ADDRESS:

LOGIN/USER:

PASSWORD:

NOTES:

SITE NAME:

WEB ADDRESS:

LOGIN/USER:

PASSWORD:

NOTES:

C

SITE NAME:

WEB ADDRESS:

LOGIN/USER:

PASSWORD:

NOTES:

SITE NAME:

WEB ADDRESS:

LOGIN/USER:

PASSWORD:

NOTES:

SITE NAME:

WEB ADDRESS:

LOGIN/USER:

PASSWORD:

NOTES:

SITE NAME:

WEB ADDRESS:

LOGIN/USER:

PASSWORD:

NOTES:

C

SITE NAME:

WEB ADDRESS:

LOGIN/USER:

PASSWORD:

NOTES:

SITE NAME:

WEB ADDRESS:

LOGIN/USER:

PASSWORD:

NOTES:

SITE NAME:

WEB ADDRESS:

LOGIN/USER:

PASSWORD:

NOTES:

SITE NAME:

WEB ADDRESS:

LOGIN/USER:

PASSWORD:

NOTES:

C

SITE NAME:

WEB ADDRESS:

LOGIN/USER:

PASSWORD:

NOTES:

SITE NAME:

WEB ADDRESS:

LOGIN/USER:

PASSWORD:

NOTES:

SITE NAME:

WEB ADDRESS:

LOGIN/USER:

PASSWORD:

NOTES:

SITE NAME:

WEB ADDRESS:

LOGIN/USER:

PASSWORD:

NOTES:

D

D

D

D

D

SITE NAME:

WEB ADDRESS:

LOGIN/USER:

PASSWORD:

NOTES:

SITE NAME:

WEB ADDRESS:

LOGIN/USER:

PASSWORD:

NOTES:

SITE NAME:

WEB ADDRESS:

LOGIN/USER:

PASSWORD:

NOTES:

SITE NAME:

WEB ADDRESS:

LOGIN/USER:

PASSWORD:

NOTES:

SITE NAME:

WEB ADDRESS:

LOGIN/USER:

PASSWORD:

NOTES:

SITE NAME:

WEB ADDRESS:

LOGIN/USER:

PASSWORD:

NOTES:

SITE NAME:

WEB ADDRESS:

LOGIN/USER:

PASSWORD:

NOTES:

SITE NAME:

WEB ADDRESS:

LOGIN/USER:

PASSWORD:

NOTES:

D

D D D D D

SITE NAME:

WEB ADDRESS:

LOGIN/USER:

PASSWORD:

NOTES:

SITE NAME:

WEB ADDRESS:

LOGIN/USER:

PASSWORD:

NOTES:

SITE NAME:

WEB ADDRESS:

LOGIN/USER:

PASSWORD:

NOTES:

SITE NAME:

WEB ADDRESS:

LOGIN/USER:

PASSWORD:

NOTES:

D D D D D

SITE NAME:

WEB ADDRESS:

LOGIN/USER:

PASSWORD:

NOTES:

SITE NAME:

WEB ADDRESS:

LOGIN/USER:

PASSWORD:

NOTES:

SITE NAME:

WEB ADDRESS:

LOGIN/USER:

PASSWORD:

NOTES:

SITE NAME:

WEB ADDRESS:

LOGIN/USER:

PASSWORD:

NOTES:

E

E

E

E

E

SITE NAME:

WEB ADDRESS:

LOGIN/USER:

PASSWORD:

NOTES:

SITE NAME:

WEB ADDRESS:

LOGIN/USER:

PASSWORD:

NOTES:

SITE NAME:

WEB ADDRESS:

LOGIN/USER:

PASSWORD:

NOTES:

SITE NAME:

WEB ADDRESS:

LOGIN/USER:

PASSWORD:

NOTES:

SITE NAME:

WEB ADDRESS:

LOGIN/USER:

PASSWORD:

NOTES:

SITE NAME:

WEB ADDRESS:

LOGIN/USER:

PASSWORD:

NOTES:

SITE NAME:

WEB ADDRESS:

LOGIN/USER:

PASSWORD:

NOTES:

SITE NAME:

WEB ADDRESS:

LOGIN/USER:

PASSWORD:

NOTES:

E

E

SITE NAME:

WEB ADDRESS:

LOGIN/USER:

PASSWORD:

NOTES:

SITE NAME:

WEB ADDRESS:

LOGIN/USER:

PASSWORD:

NOTES:

SITE NAME:

WEB ADDRESS:

LOGIN/USER:

PASSWORD:

NOTES:

SITE NAME:

WEB ADDRESS:

LOGIN/USER:

PASSWORD:

NOTES:

E

E

E

E

E

SITE NAME:

WEB ADDRESS:

LOGIN/USER:

PASSWORD:

NOTES:

SITE NAME:

WEB ADDRESS:

LOGIN/USER:

PASSWORD:

NOTES:

SITE NAME:

WEB ADDRESS:

LOGIN/USER:

PASSWORD:

NOTES:

SITE NAME:

WEB ADDRESS:

LOGIN/USER:

PASSWORD:

NOTES:

F

SITE NAME:

WEB ADDRESS:

LOGIN/USER:

PASSWORD:

NOTES:

SITE NAME:

WEB ADDRESS:

LOGIN/USER:

PASSWORD:

NOTES:

SITE NAME:

WEB ADDRESS:

LOGIN/USER:

PASSWORD:

NOTES:

SITE NAME:

WEB ADDRESS:

LOGIN/USER:

PASSWORD:

NOTES:

F

SITE NAME:

WEB ADDRESS:

LOGIN/USER:

PASSWORD:

NOTES:

SITE NAME:

WEB ADDRESS:

LOGIN/USER:

PASSWORD:

NOTES:

SITE NAME:

WEB ADDRESS:

LOGIN/USER:

PASSWORD:

NOTES:

SITE NAME:

WEB ADDRESS:

LOGIN/USER:

PASSWORD:

NOTES:

F F F F F

SITE NAME:

WEB ADDRESS:

LOGIN/USER:

PASSWORD:

NOTES:

SITE NAME:

WEB ADDRESS:

LOGIN/USER:

PASSWORD:

NOTES:

SITE NAME:

WEB ADDRESS:

LOGIN/USER:

PASSWORD:

NOTES:

SITE NAME:

WEB ADDRESS:

LOGIN/USER:

PASSWORD:

NOTES:

F

SITE NAME:

WEB ADDRESS:

LOGIN/USER:

PASSWORD:

NOTES:

SITE NAME:

WEB ADDRESS:

LOGIN/USER:

PASSWORD:

NOTES:

SITE NAME:

WEB ADDRESS:

LOGIN/USER:

PASSWORD:

NOTES:

SITE NAME:

WEB ADDRESS:

LOGIN/USER:

PASSWORD:

NOTES:

G

G

G

G

G

SITE NAME:

WEB ADDRESS:

LOGIN/USER:

PASSWORD:

NOTES:

SITE NAME:

WEB ADDRESS:

LOGIN/USER:

PASSWORD:

NOTES:

SITE NAME:

WEB ADDRESS:

LOGIN/USER:

PASSWORD:

NOTES:

SITE NAME:

WEB ADDRESS:

LOGIN/USER:

PASSWORD:

NOTES:

G G G G G

SITE NAME:
WEB ADDRESS:
LOGIN/USER:
PASSWORD:

NOTES:

SITE NAME:
WEB ADDRESS:
LOGIN/USER:
PASSWORD:

NOTES:

SITE NAME:
WEB ADDRESS:
LOGIN/USER:
PASSWORD:

NOTES:

SITE NAME:
WEB ADDRESS:
LOGIN/USER:
PASSWORD:

NOTES:

G G G G G

SITE NAME:

WEB ADDRESS:

LOGIN/USER:

PASSWORD:

NOTES:

SITE NAME:

WEB ADDRESS:

LOGIN/USER:

PASSWORD:

NOTES:

SITE NAME:

WEB ADDRESS:

LOGIN/USER:

PASSWORD:

NOTES:

SITE NAME:

WEB ADDRESS:

LOGIN/USER:

PASSWORD:

NOTES:

G G G G G

SITE NAME:

WEB ADDRESS:

LOGIN/USER:

PASSWORD:

NOTES:

SITE NAME:

WEB ADDRESS:

LOGIN/USER:

PASSWORD:

NOTES:

SITE NAME:

WEB ADDRESS:

LOGIN/USER:

PASSWORD:

NOTES:

SITE NAME:

WEB ADDRESS:

LOGIN/USER:

PASSWORD:

NOTES:

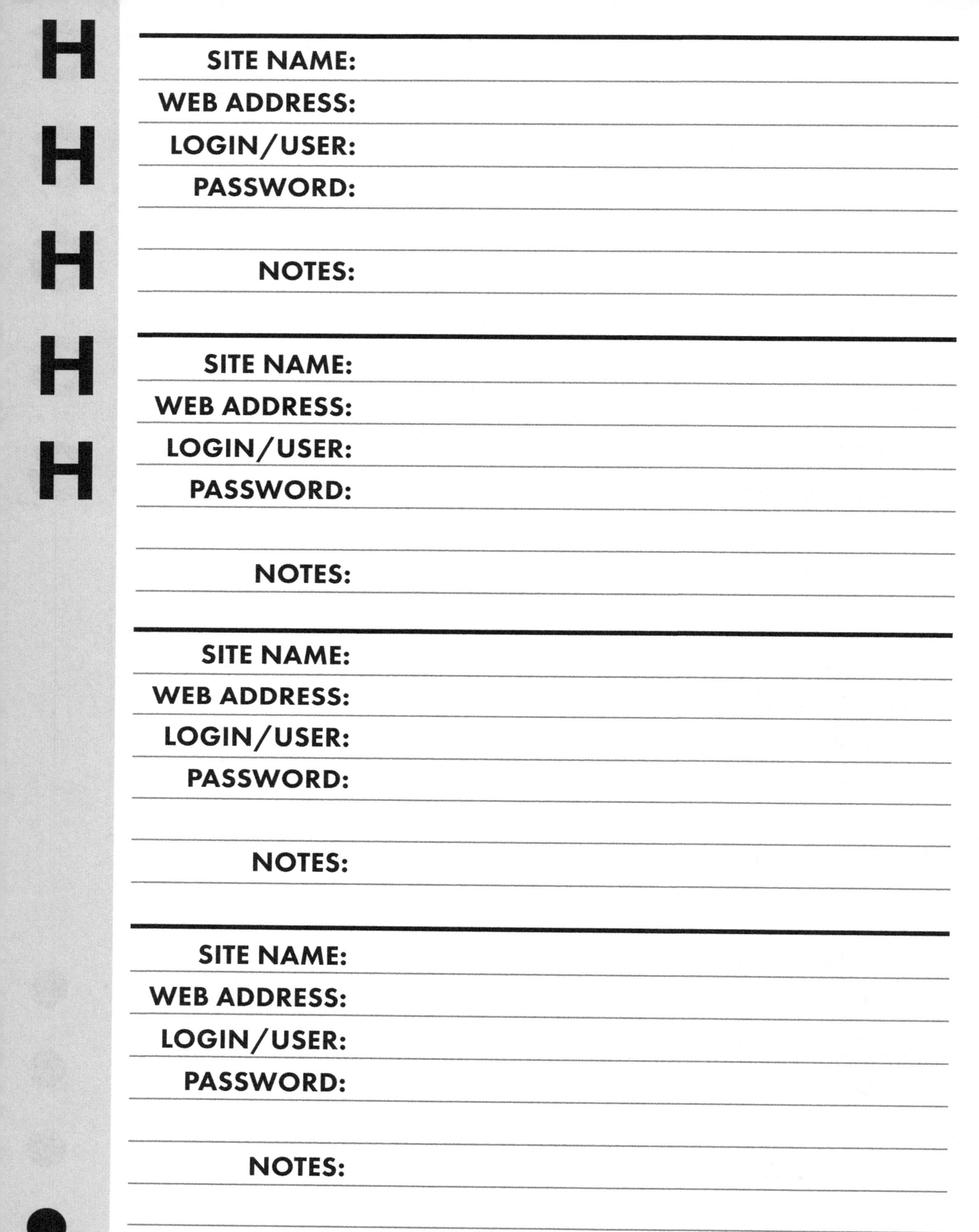
H
H
H
H
H
SITE NAME:
WEB ADDRESS:
LOGIN/USER:
PASSWORD:
NOTES:
SITE NAME:
WEB ADDRESS:
LOGIN/USER:
PASSWORD:
NOTES:
SITE NAME:
WEB ADDRESS:
LOGIN/USER:
PASSWORD:
NOTES:
SITE NAME:
WEB ADDRESS:
LOGIN/USER:
PASSWORD:
NOTES:

H

SITE NAME:

WEB ADDRESS:

LOGIN/USER:

PASSWORD:

NOTES:

SITE NAME:

WEB ADDRESS:

LOGIN/USER:

PASSWORD:

NOTES:

SITE NAME:

WEB ADDRESS:

LOGIN/USER:

PASSWORD:

NOTES:

SITE NAME:

WEB ADDRESS:

LOGIN/USER:

PASSWORD:

NOTES:

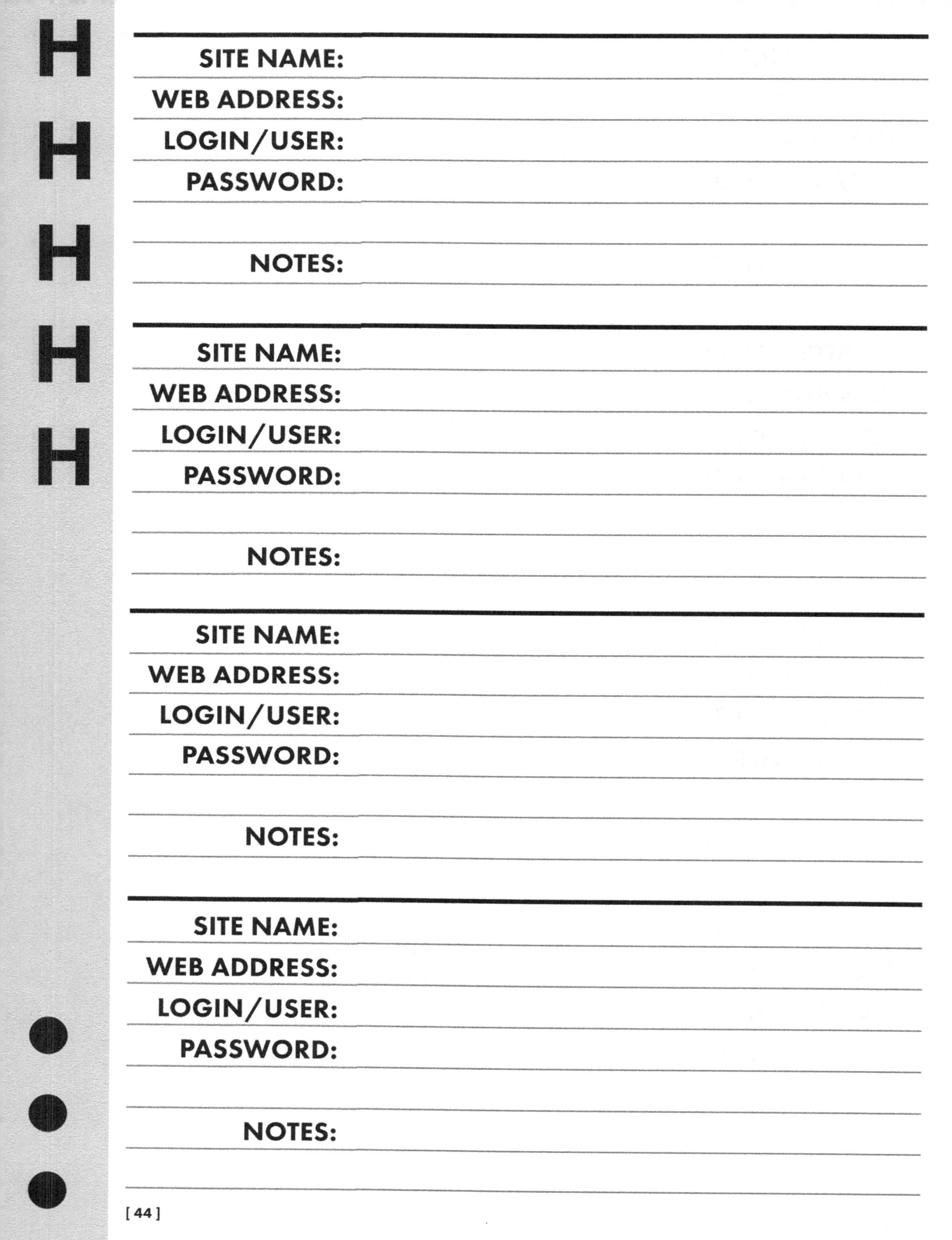

H

SITE NAME:

WEB ADDRESS:

LOGIN/USER:

PASSWORD:

NOTES:

SITE NAME:

WEB ADDRESS:

LOGIN/USER:

PASSWORD:

NOTES:

SITE NAME:

WEB ADDRESS:

LOGIN/USER:

PASSWORD:

NOTES:

SITE NAME:

WEB ADDRESS:

LOGIN/USER:

PASSWORD:

NOTES:

H H H H H

SITE NAME:

WEB ADDRESS:

LOGIN/USER:

PASSWORD:

NOTES:

SITE NAME:

WEB ADDRESS:

LOGIN/USER:

PASSWORD:

NOTES:

SITE NAME:

WEB ADDRESS:

LOGIN/USER:

PASSWORD:

NOTES:

SITE NAME:

WEB ADDRESS:

LOGIN/USER:

PASSWORD:

NOTES:

H H H H H

SITE NAME:

WEB ADDRESS:

LOGIN/USER:

PASSWORD:

NOTES:

SITE NAME:

WEB ADDRESS:

LOGIN/USER:

PASSWORD:

NOTES:

SITE NAME:

WEB ADDRESS:

LOGIN/USER:

PASSWORD:

NOTES:

SITE NAME:

WEB ADDRESS:

LOGIN/USER:

PASSWORD:

NOTES:

SITE NAME:

WEB ADDRESS:

LOGIN/USER:

PASSWORD:

NOTES:

SITE NAME:

WEB ADDRESS:

LOGIN/USER:

PASSWORD:

NOTES:

SITE NAME:

WEB ADDRESS:

LOGIN/USER:

PASSWORD:

NOTES:

SITE NAME:

WEB ADDRESS:

LOGIN/USER:

PASSWORD:

NOTES:

H

SITE NAME:

WEB ADDRESS:

LOGIN/USER:

PASSWORD:

NOTES:

SITE NAME:

WEB ADDRESS:

LOGIN/USER:

PASSWORD:

NOTES:

SITE NAME:

WEB ADDRESS:

LOGIN/USER:

PASSWORD:

NOTES:

SITE NAME:

WEB ADDRESS:

LOGIN/USER:

PASSWORD:

NOTES:

SITE NAME:
WEB ADDRESS:
LOGIN/USER:
PASSWORD:

NOTES:

SITE NAME:
WEB ADDRESS:
LOGIN/USER:
PASSWORD:

NOTES:

SITE NAME:
WEB ADDRESS:
LOGIN/USER:
PASSWORD:

NOTES:

SITE NAME:
WEB ADDRESS:
LOGIN/USER:
PASSWORD:

NOTES:

J J J J J

SITE NAME:

WEB ADDRESS:

LOGIN/USER:

PASSWORD:

NOTES:

SITE NAME:

WEB ADDRESS:

LOGIN/USER:

PASSWORD:

NOTES:

SITE NAME:

WEB ADDRESS:

LOGIN/USER:

PASSWORD:

NOTES:

SITE NAME:

WEB ADDRESS:

LOGIN/USER:

PASSWORD:

NOTES:

SITE NAME:

WEB ADDRESS:

LOGIN/USER:

PASSWORD:

NOTES:

SITE NAME:

WEB ADDRESS:

LOGIN/USER:

PASSWORD:

NOTES:

SITE NAME:

WEB ADDRESS:

LOGIN/USER:

PASSWORD:

NOTES:

SITE NAME:

WEB ADDRESS:

LOGIN/USER:

PASSWORD:

NOTES:

J J J J J

K

K

K

K

K

SITE NAME:

WEB ADDRESS:

LOGIN/USER:

PASSWORD:

NOTES:

SITE NAME:

WEB ADDRESS:

LOGIN/USER:

PASSWORD:

NOTES:

SITE NAME:

WEB ADDRESS:

LOGIN/USER:

PASSWORD:

NOTES:

SITE NAME:

WEB ADDRESS:

LOGIN/USER:

PASSWORD:

NOTES:

SITE NAME:

WEB ADDRESS:

LOGIN/USER:

PASSWORD:

NOTES:

SITE NAME:

WEB ADDRESS:

LOGIN/USER:

PASSWORD:

NOTES:

SITE NAME:

WEB ADDRESS:

LOGIN/USER:

PASSWORD:

NOTES:

SITE NAME:

WEB ADDRESS:

LOGIN/USER:

PASSWORD:

NOTES:

K K K K K

L

SITE NAME:

WEB ADDRESS:

LOGIN/USER:

PASSWORD:

NOTES:

SITE NAME:

WEB ADDRESS:

LOGIN/USER:

PASSWORD:

NOTES:

SITE NAME:

WEB ADDRESS:

LOGIN/USER:

PASSWORD:

NOTES:

SITE NAME:

WEB ADDRESS:

LOGIN/USER:

PASSWORD:

NOTES:

SITE NAME:

WEB ADDRESS:

LOGIN/USER:

PASSWORD:

NOTES:

SITE NAME:

WEB ADDRESS:

LOGIN/USER:

PASSWORD:

NOTES:

SITE NAME:

WEB ADDRESS:

LOGIN/USER:

PASSWORD:

NOTES:

SITE NAME:

WEB ADDRESS:

LOGIN/USER:

PASSWORD:

NOTES:

L

L

SITE NAME:

WEB ADDRESS:

LOGIN/USER:

PASSWORD:

NOTES:

SITE NAME:

WEB ADDRESS:

LOGIN/USER:

PASSWORD:

NOTES:

SITE NAME:

WEB ADDRESS:

LOGIN/USER:

PASSWORD:

NOTES:

SITE NAME:

WEB ADDRESS:

LOGIN/USER:

PASSWORD:

NOTES:

SITE NAME:

WEB ADDRESS:

LOGIN/USER:

PASSWORD:

NOTES:

SITE NAME:

WEB ADDRESS:

LOGIN/USER:

PASSWORD:

NOTES:

SITE NAME:

WEB ADDRESS:

LOGIN/USER:

PASSWORD:

NOTES:

SITE NAME:

WEB ADDRESS:

LOGIN/USER:

PASSWORD:

NOTES:

M M M M M

SITE NAME:

WEB ADDRESS:

LOGIN/USER:

PASSWORD:

NOTES:

SITE NAME:

WEB ADDRESS:

LOGIN/USER:

PASSWORD:

NOTES:

SITE NAME:

WEB ADDRESS:

LOGIN/USER:

PASSWORD:

NOTES:

SITE NAME:

WEB ADDRESS:

LOGIN/USER:

PASSWORD:

NOTES:

SITE NAME:

WEB ADDRESS:

LOGIN/USER:

PASSWORD:

NOTES:

SITE NAME:

WEB ADDRESS:

LOGIN/USER:

PASSWORD:

NOTES:

SITE NAME:

WEB ADDRESS:

LOGIN/USER:

PASSWORD:

NOTES:

SITE NAME:

WEB ADDRESS:

LOGIN/USER:

PASSWORD:

NOTES:

M

M

M

M

M

SITE NAME:

WEB ADDRESS:

LOGIN/USER:

PASSWORD:

NOTES:

SITE NAME:

WEB ADDRESS:

LOGIN/USER:

PASSWORD:

NOTES:

SITE NAME:

WEB ADDRESS:

LOGIN/USER:

PASSWORD:

NOTES:

SITE NAME:

WEB ADDRESS:

LOGIN/USER:

PASSWORD:

NOTES:

M

SITE NAME:

WEB ADDRESS:

LOGIN/USER:

PASSWORD:

NOTES:

SITE NAME:

WEB ADDRESS:

LOGIN/USER:

PASSWORD:

NOTES:

SITE NAME:

WEB ADDRESS:

LOGIN/USER:

PASSWORD:

NOTES:

SITE NAME:

WEB ADDRESS:

LOGIN/USER:

PASSWORD:

NOTES:

M

SITE NAME:

WEB ADDRESS:

LOGIN/USER:

PASSWORD:

NOTES:

SITE NAME:

WEB ADDRESS:

LOGIN/USER:

PASSWORD:

NOTES:

SITE NAME:

WEB ADDRESS:

LOGIN/USER:

PASSWORD:

NOTES:

SITE NAME:

WEB ADDRESS:

LOGIN/USER:

PASSWORD:

NOTES:

SITE NAME:

WEB ADDRESS:

LOGIN/USER:

PASSWORD:

NOTES:

SITE NAME:

WEB ADDRESS:

LOGIN/USER:

PASSWORD:

NOTES:

SITE NAME:

WEB ADDRESS:

LOGIN/USER:

PASSWORD:

NOTES:

SITE NAME:

WEB ADDRESS:

LOGIN/USER:

PASSWORD:

NOTES:

N
N
N
N
N

SITE NAME:

WEB ADDRESS:

LOGIN/USER:

PASSWORD:

NOTES:

SITE NAME:

WEB ADDRESS:

LOGIN/USER:

PASSWORD:

NOTES:

SITE NAME:

WEB ADDRESS:

LOGIN/USER:

PASSWORD:

NOTES:

SITE NAME:

WEB ADDRESS:

LOGIN/USER:

PASSWORD:

NOTES:

N

SITE NAME:

WEB ADDRESS:

LOGIN/USER:

PASSWORD:

NOTES:

SITE NAME:

WEB ADDRESS:

LOGIN/USER:

PASSWORD:

NOTES:

SITE NAME:

WEB ADDRESS:

LOGIN/USER:

PASSWORD:

NOTES:

SITE NAME:

WEB ADDRESS:

LOGIN/USER:

PASSWORD:

NOTES:

N N N N N

SITE NAME:

WEB ADDRESS:

LOGIN/USER:

PASSWORD:

NOTES:

SITE NAME:

WEB ADDRESS:

LOGIN/USER:

PASSWORD:

NOTES:

SITE NAME:

WEB ADDRESS:

LOGIN/USER:

PASSWORD:

NOTES:

SITE NAME:

WEB ADDRESS:

LOGIN/USER:

PASSWORD:

NOTES:

N

SITE NAME:

WEB ADDRESS:

LOGIN/USER:

PASSWORD:

NOTES:

SITE NAME:

WEB ADDRESS:

LOGIN/USER:

PASSWORD:

NOTES:

SITE NAME:

WEB ADDRESS:

LOGIN/USER:

PASSWORD:

NOTES:

SITE NAME:

WEB ADDRESS:

LOGIN/USER:

PASSWORD:

NOTES:

SITE NAME:

WEB ADDRESS:

LOGIN/USER:

PASSWORD:

NOTES:

SITE NAME:

WEB ADDRESS:

LOGIN/USER:

PASSWORD:

NOTES:

SITE NAME:

WEB ADDRESS:

LOGIN/USER:

PASSWORD:

NOTES:

SITE NAME:

WEB ADDRESS:

LOGIN/USER:

PASSWORD:

NOTES:

SITE NAME:
WEB ADDRESS:
LOGIN/USER:
PASSWORD:

NOTES:

SITE NAME:
WEB ADDRESS:
LOGIN/USER:
PASSWORD:

NOTES:

SITE NAME:
WEB ADDRESS:
LOGIN/USER:
PASSWORD:

NOTES:

SITE NAME:
WEB ADDRESS:
LOGIN/USER:
PASSWORD:

NOTES:

P P P P P

SITE NAME:

WEB ADDRESS:

LOGIN/USER:

PASSWORD:

NOTES:

SITE NAME:

WEB ADDRESS:

LOGIN/USER:

PASSWORD:

NOTES:

SITE NAME:

WEB ADDRESS:

LOGIN/USER:

PASSWORD:

NOTES:

SITE NAME:

WEB ADDRESS:

LOGIN/USER:

PASSWORD:

NOTES:

SITE NAME:

WEB ADDRESS:

LOGIN/USER:

PASSWORD:

NOTES:

SITE NAME:

WEB ADDRESS:

LOGIN/USER:

PASSWORD:

NOTES:

SITE NAME:

WEB ADDRESS:

LOGIN/USER:

PASSWORD:

NOTES:

SITE NAME:

WEB ADDRESS:

LOGIN/USER:

PASSWORD:

NOTES:

P

SITE NAME:

WEB ADDRESS:

LOGIN/USER:

PASSWORD:

NOTES:

SITE NAME:

WEB ADDRESS:

LOGIN/USER:

PASSWORD:

NOTES:

SITE NAME:

WEB ADDRESS:

LOGIN/USER:

PASSWORD:

NOTES:

SITE NAME:

WEB ADDRESS:

LOGIN/USER:

PASSWORD:

NOTES:

P

SITE NAME:

WEB ADDRESS:

LOGIN/USER:

PASSWORD:

NOTES:

SITE NAME:

WEB ADDRESS:

LOGIN/USER:

PASSWORD:

NOTES:

SITE NAME:

WEB ADDRESS:

LOGIN/USER:

PASSWORD:

NOTES:

SITE NAME:

WEB ADDRESS:

LOGIN/USER:

PASSWORD:

NOTES:

P

SITE NAME:

WEB ADDRESS:

LOGIN/USER:

PASSWORD:

NOTES:

SITE NAME:

WEB ADDRESS:

LOGIN/USER:

PASSWORD:

NOTES:

SITE NAME:

WEB ADDRESS:

LOGIN/USER:

PASSWORD:

NOTES:

SITE NAME:

WEB ADDRESS:

LOGIN/USER:

PASSWORD:

NOTES:

P

P

P

P

P

SITE NAME:

WEB ADDRESS:

LOGIN/USER:

PASSWORD:

NOTES:

SITE NAME:

WEB ADDRESS:

LOGIN/USER:

PASSWORD:

NOTES:

SITE NAME:

WEB ADDRESS:

LOGIN/USER:

PASSWORD:

NOTES:

SITE NAME:

WEB ADDRESS:

LOGIN/USER:

PASSWORD:

NOTES:

Q
Q
Q
Q
Q

SITE NAME:
WEB ADDRESS:
LOGIN/USER:
PASSWORD:

NOTES:

SITE NAME:
WEB ADDRESS:
LOGIN/USER:
PASSWORD:

NOTES:

SITE NAME:
WEB ADDRESS:
LOGIN/USER:
PASSWORD:

NOTES:

SITE NAME:
WEB ADDRESS:
LOGIN/USER:
PASSWORD:

NOTES:

SITE NAME:

WEB ADDRESS:

LOGIN/USER:

PASSWORD:

NOTES:

SITE NAME:

WEB ADDRESS:

LOGIN/USER:

PASSWORD:

NOTES:

SITE NAME:

WEB ADDRESS:

LOGIN/USER:

PASSWORD:

NOTES:

SITE NAME:

WEB ADDRESS:

LOGIN/USER:

PASSWORD:

NOTES:

Q Q Q Q Q

R

SITE NAME:

WEB ADDRESS:

LOGIN/USER:

PASSWORD:

NOTES:

SITE NAME:

WEB ADDRESS:

LOGIN/USER:

PASSWORD:

NOTES:

SITE NAME:

WEB ADDRESS:

LOGIN/USER:

PASSWORD:

NOTES:

SITE NAME:

WEB ADDRESS:

LOGIN/USER:

PASSWORD:

NOTES:

SITE NAME:

WEB ADDRESS:

LOGIN/USER:

PASSWORD:

NOTES:

SITE NAME:

WEB ADDRESS:

LOGIN/USER:

PASSWORD:

NOTES:

SITE NAME:

WEB ADDRESS:

LOGIN/USER:

PASSWORD:

NOTES:

SITE NAME:

WEB ADDRESS:

LOGIN/USER:

PASSWORD:

NOTES:

R

R

SITE NAME:

WEB ADDRESS:

LOGIN/USER:

PASSWORD:

NOTES:

SITE NAME:

WEB ADDRESS:

LOGIN/USER:

PASSWORD:

NOTES:

SITE NAME:

WEB ADDRESS:

LOGIN/USER:

PASSWORD:

NOTES:

SITE NAME:

WEB ADDRESS:

LOGIN/USER:

PASSWORD:

NOTES:

R R R R R

SITE NAME:

WEB ADDRESS:

LOGIN/USER:

PASSWORD:

NOTES:

SITE NAME:

WEB ADDRESS:

LOGIN/USER:

PASSWORD:

NOTES:

SITE NAME:

WEB ADDRESS:

LOGIN/USER:

PASSWORD:

NOTES:

SITE NAME:

WEB ADDRESS:

LOGIN/USER:

PASSWORD:

NOTES:

R R R R R

SITE NAME:

WEB ADDRESS:

LOGIN/USER:

PASSWORD:

NOTES:

SITE NAME:

WEB ADDRESS:

LOGIN/USER:

PASSWORD:

NOTES:

SITE NAME:

WEB ADDRESS:

LOGIN/USER:

PASSWORD:

NOTES:

SITE NAME:

WEB ADDRESS:

LOGIN/USER:

PASSWORD:

NOTES:

R

SITE NAME:

WEB ADDRESS:

LOGIN/USER:

PASSWORD:

NOTES:

SITE NAME:

WEB ADDRESS:

LOGIN/USER:

PASSWORD:

NOTES:

SITE NAME:

WEB ADDRESS:

LOGIN/USER:

PASSWORD:

NOTES:

SITE NAME:

WEB ADDRESS:

LOGIN/USER:

PASSWORD:

NOTES:

S

SITE NAME:

WEB ADDRESS:

LOGIN/USER:

PASSWORD:

NOTES:

SITE NAME:

WEB ADDRESS:

LOGIN/USER:

PASSWORD:

NOTES:

SITE NAME:

WEB ADDRESS:

LOGIN/USER:

PASSWORD:

NOTES:

SITE NAME:

WEB ADDRESS:

LOGIN/USER:

PASSWORD:

NOTES:

S

SITE NAME:

WEB ADDRESS:

LOGIN/USER:

PASSWORD:

NOTES:

SITE NAME:

WEB ADDRESS:

LOGIN/USER:

PASSWORD:

NOTES:

SITE NAME:

WEB ADDRESS:

LOGIN/USER:

PASSWORD:

NOTES:

SITE NAME:

WEB ADDRESS:

LOGIN/USER:

PASSWORD:

NOTES:

S

SITE NAME:

WEB ADDRESS:

LOGIN/USER:

PASSWORD:

NOTES:

SITE NAME:

WEB ADDRESS:

LOGIN/USER:

PASSWORD:

NOTES:

SITE NAME:

WEB ADDRESS:

LOGIN/USER:

PASSWORD:

NOTES:

SITE NAME:

WEB ADDRESS:

LOGIN/USER:

PASSWORD:

NOTES:

S S S S S

SITE NAME:

WEB ADDRESS:

LOGIN/USER:

PASSWORD:

NOTES:

SITE NAME:

WEB ADDRESS:

LOGIN/USER:

PASSWORD:

NOTES:

SITE NAME:

WEB ADDRESS:

LOGIN/USER:

PASSWORD:

NOTES:

SITE NAME:

WEB ADDRESS:

LOGIN/USER:

PASSWORD:

NOTES:

S
S
S
S
S

SITE NAME:
WEB ADDRESS:
LOGIN/USER:
PASSWORD:

NOTES:

SITE NAME:
WEB ADDRESS:
LOGIN/USER:
PASSWORD:

NOTES:

SITE NAME:
WEB ADDRESS:
LOGIN/USER:
PASSWORD:

NOTES:

SITE NAME:
WEB ADDRESS:
LOGIN/USER:
PASSWORD:

NOTES:

S S S S S

SITE NAME:

WEB ADDRESS:

LOGIN/USER:

PASSWORD:

NOTES:

SITE NAME:

WEB ADDRESS:

LOGIN/USER:

PASSWORD:

NOTES:

SITE NAME:

WEB ADDRESS:

LOGIN/USER:

PASSWORD:

NOTES:

SITE NAME:

WEB ADDRESS:

LOGIN/USER:

PASSWORD:

NOTES:

T

SITE NAME:

WEB ADDRESS:

LOGIN/USER:

PASSWORD:

NOTES:

SITE NAME:

WEB ADDRESS:

LOGIN/USER:

PASSWORD:

NOTES:

SITE NAME:

WEB ADDRESS:

LOGIN/USER:

PASSWORD:

NOTES:

SITE NAME:

WEB ADDRESS:

LOGIN/USER:

PASSWORD:

NOTES:

SITE NAME:

WEB ADDRESS:

LOGIN/USER:

PASSWORD:

NOTES:

SITE NAME:

WEB ADDRESS:

LOGIN/USER:

PASSWORD:

NOTES:

SITE NAME:

WEB ADDRESS:

LOGIN/USER:

PASSWORD:

NOTES:

SITE NAME:

WEB ADDRESS:

LOGIN/USER:

PASSWORD:

NOTES:

SITE NAME:

WEB ADDRESS:

LOGIN/USER:

PASSWORD:

NOTES:

SITE NAME:

WEB ADDRESS:

LOGIN/USER:

PASSWORD:

NOTES:

SITE NAME:

WEB ADDRESS:

LOGIN/USER:

PASSWORD:

NOTES:

SITE NAME:

WEB ADDRESS:

LOGIN/USER:

PASSWORD:

NOTES:

T

SITE NAME:

WEB ADDRESS:

LOGIN/USER:

PASSWORD:

NOTES:

SITE NAME:

WEB ADDRESS:

LOGIN/USER:

PASSWORD:

NOTES:

SITE NAME:

WEB ADDRESS:

LOGIN/USER:

PASSWORD:

NOTES:

SITE NAME:

WEB ADDRESS:

LOGIN/USER:

PASSWORD:

NOTES:

T

SITE NAME:

WEB ADDRESS:

LOGIN/USER:

PASSWORD:

NOTES:

SITE NAME:

WEB ADDRESS:

LOGIN/USER:

PASSWORD:

NOTES:

SITE NAME:

WEB ADDRESS:

LOGIN/USER:

PASSWORD:

NOTES:

SITE NAME:

WEB ADDRESS:

LOGIN/USER:

PASSWORD:

NOTES:

T

SITE NAME:

WEB ADDRESS:

LOGIN/USER:

PASSWORD:

NOTES:

SITE NAME:

WEB ADDRESS:

LOGIN/USER:

PASSWORD:

NOTES:

SITE NAME:

WEB ADDRESS:

LOGIN/USER:

PASSWORD:

NOTES:

SITE NAME:

WEB ADDRESS:

LOGIN/USER:

PASSWORD:

NOTES:

U

V

SITE NAME:

WEB ADDRESS:

LOGIN/USER:

PASSWORD:

NOTES:

SITE NAME:

WEB ADDRESS:

LOGIN/USER:

PASSWORD:

NOTES:

SITE NAME:

WEB ADDRESS:

LOGIN/USER:

PASSWORD:

NOTES:

SITE NAME:

WEB ADDRESS:

LOGIN/USER:

PASSWORD:

NOTES:

SITE NAME:

WEB ADDRESS:

LOGIN/USER:

PASSWORD:

NOTES:

SITE NAME:

WEB ADDRESS:

LOGIN/USER:

PASSWORD:

NOTES:

SITE NAME:

WEB ADDRESS:

LOGIN/USER:

PASSWORD:

NOTES:

SITE NAME:

WEB ADDRESS:

LOGIN/USER:

PASSWORD:

NOTES:

U
V

SITE NAME:

WEB ADDRESS:

LOGIN/USER:

PASSWORD:

NOTES:

U
V

SITE NAME:

WEB ADDRESS:

LOGIN/USER:

PASSWORD:

NOTES:

SITE NAME:

WEB ADDRESS:

LOGIN/USER:

PASSWORD:

NOTES:

SITE NAME:

WEB ADDRESS:

LOGIN/USER:

PASSWORD:

NOTES:

SITE NAME:

WEB ADDRESS:

LOGIN/USER:

PASSWORD:

NOTES:

SITE NAME:

WEB ADDRESS:

LOGIN/USER:

PASSWORD:

NOTES:

SITE NAME:

WEB ADDRESS:

LOGIN/USER:

PASSWORD:

NOTES:

SITE NAME:

WEB ADDRESS:

LOGIN/USER:

PASSWORD:

NOTES:

W
W
W
W
W

SITE NAME:

WEB ADDRESS:

LOGIN/USER:

PASSWORD:

NOTES:

SITE NAME:

WEB ADDRESS:

LOGIN/USER:

PASSWORD:

NOTES:

SITE NAME:

WEB ADDRESS:

LOGIN/USER:

PASSWORD:

NOTES:

SITE NAME:

WEB ADDRESS:

LOGIN/USER:

PASSWORD:

NOTES:

W W W W W

SITE NAME:

WEB ADDRESS:

LOGIN/USER:

PASSWORD:

NOTES:

SITE NAME:

WEB ADDRESS:

LOGIN/USER:

PASSWORD:

NOTES:

SITE NAME:

WEB ADDRESS:

LOGIN/USER:

PASSWORD:

NOTES:

SITE NAME:

WEB ADDRESS:

LOGIN/USER:

PASSWORD:

NOTES:

W

W

W

W

W

SITE NAME:

WEB ADDRESS:

LOGIN/USER:

PASSWORD:

NOTES:

SITE NAME:

WEB ADDRESS:

LOGIN/USER:

PASSWORD:

NOTES:

SITE NAME:

WEB ADDRESS:

LOGIN/USER:

PASSWORD:

NOTES:

SITE NAME:

WEB ADDRESS:

LOGIN/USER:

PASSWORD:

NOTES:

W

SITE NAME:

WEB ADDRESS:

LOGIN/USER:

PASSWORD:

NOTES:

SITE NAME:

WEB ADDRESS:

LOGIN/USER:

PASSWORD:

NOTES:

SITE NAME:

WEB ADDRESS:

LOGIN/USER:

PASSWORD:

NOTES:

SITE NAME:

WEB ADDRESS:

LOGIN/USER:

PASSWORD:

NOTES:

W

W

W

W

W

SITE NAME:

WEB ADDRESS:

LOGIN/USER:

PASSWORD:

NOTES:

SITE NAME:

WEB ADDRESS:

LOGIN/USER:

PASSWORD:

NOTES:

SITE NAME:

WEB ADDRESS:

LOGIN/USER:

PASSWORD:

NOTES:

SITE NAME:

WEB ADDRESS:

LOGIN/USER:

PASSWORD:

NOTES:

W W W W W

SITE NAME:

WEB ADDRESS:

LOGIN/USER:

PASSWORD:

NOTES:

SITE NAME:

WEB ADDRESS:

LOGIN/USER:

PASSWORD:

NOTES:

SITE NAME:

WEB ADDRESS:

LOGIN/USER:

PASSWORD:

NOTES:

SITE NAME:

WEB ADDRESS:

LOGIN/USER:

PASSWORD:

NOTES:

X Y Z X Y Z

SITE NAME:

WEB ADDRESS:

LOGIN/USER:

PASSWORD:

NOTES:

SITE NAME:

WEB ADDRESS:

LOGIN/USER:

PASSWORD:

NOTES:

SITE NAME:

WEB ADDRESS:

LOGIN/USER:

PASSWORD:

NOTES:

SITE NAME:

WEB ADDRESS:

LOGIN/USER:

PASSWORD:

NOTES:

SITE NAME:

WEB ADDRESS:

LOGIN/USER:

PASSWORD:

NOTES:

SITE NAME:

WEB ADDRESS:

LOGIN/USER:

PASSWORD:

NOTES:

SITE NAME:

WEB ADDRESS:

LOGIN/USER:

PASSWORD:

NOTES:

SITE NAME:

WEB ADDRESS:

LOGIN/USER:

PASSWORD:

NOTES:

X Y Z

SITE NAME:

WEB ADDRESS:

LOGIN/USER:

PASSWORD:

NOTES:

SITE NAME:

WEB ADDRESS:

LOGIN/USER:

PASSWORD:

NOTES:

SITE NAME:

WEB ADDRESS:

LOGIN/USER:

PASSWORD:

NOTES:

SITE NAME:

WEB ADDRESS:

LOGIN/USER:

PASSWORD:

NOTES:

SITE NAME:

WEB ADDRESS:

LOGIN/USER:

PASSWORD:

NOTES:

SITE NAME:

WEB ADDRESS:

LOGIN/USER:

PASSWORD:

NOTES:

SITE NAME:

WEB ADDRESS:

LOGIN/USER:

PASSWORD:

NOTES:

SITE NAME:

WEB ADDRESS:

LOGIN/USER:

PASSWORD:

NOTES:

NOTES

LARGE PRINT PASSWORD LOGBOOK
INTERNET LOGIN & PASSWORD ORGANIZER

PUBLISHED BY SYNCHRONISTA LLC – GILBERT, ARIZONA, USA
SYNCHRONISTA® IS A REGISTERED TRADEMARK OF SYNCHRONISTA LLC
WEB: SYNCHRONISTA.COM

LOOKING FOR MORE?

ALSO FROM SYNCHRONISTA:

Large Print Address Books (4 volumes)
The Square Journal: Dot Grid Book & Bullet Planner
Large Print Adult Coloring Books (4 volumes)
Large Print Word Search Puzzles (2 volumes)
Vintage Women: Adult Coloring Book series
... and many more available at Myria.com/shop

WE HAVE WEBSITES, TOO...

ClickAmericana.com: Thousands of articles, news stories, vintage memorabilia and photos from throughout American history.

PrintColorFun.com: Hundreds of free coloring pages to download and print at home.

Myria.com: Smart stuff for real life: Health, parenting, psychology, science, tech, entertainment — plus recipes, home decor & other good things.

If you enjoyed this book, please leave a review online — and tell a friend!

SEE OTHER BOOKS AT MYRIA.COM/SHOP !

Made in the USA
Coppell, TX
05 April 2020